# THE FATAL FOOTBALL

And Other Stories

The Pupils of Langley Academy

# THE AUTHORS

**Year 7**
Billy
Chloe
Liam
Jaiden
Lois
Rayan
Ryan
Salahuddin
Sienna
Sophie
Zara

**Year 8**
Adam
Alex
Amir
Brooke
Hassan
Ishaq
Jayden
John
Jessica
Leah
Maksymillian

Riley

**Year 9**
Kalimullah
Katrina
Lacey-Mae
Marcel
Maya
Osamagbee
Rachel
Raheem
Saif
Tyrone
Yousef

# CONTENTS

Title Page
The Authors
Foreword
Alien Attack ............................................................. 1
The Little Boy from Lahore ................................... 7
The Boy Called Ishak Guizem: Trust the Process ... 11
Foul Play ................................................................. 17
The Phantom Footballer ........................................ 23
The Fatal Football .................................................. 25
The Greatest Game ................................................ 30
Taking it to TikTok ................................................. 32
The Biased Referee ................................................ 38
Going Big in Brazil ................................................. 40
The Librarian's Revenge ........................................ 43
Fighting Fire with Fire ........................................... 50
The Ball Apocalypse ............................................... 54
The Switch .............................................................. 57
The Dylan Case ....................................................... 63
Acknowledgement ................................................. 73
More Information .................................................. 75

# FOREWORD

When Seth Burkett came to spend World Book Day with us in 2022, he was a huge and instant hit. His friendly, laidback demeanour, his inspirational assemblies, and his enthusiasm for both reading, writing AND football was an irresistible combination, not to mention his willingness to join the students in a kickabout at lunchtime, and I wasted no time in asking him to be the Langley Academy's first Author in Residence for the year.

This book is the outcome of just some of the work Seth has done with our students over the past academic year and we are really proud of it! It's not always easy turning enthusiasm for a sport into convincing stories, and indeed not all the stories in this book are about football, but it remains the main theme. Murder and mystery abound! Aliens save the day on the pitch, and a spat on TikTok goes viral! Some boys achieve their biggest dreams, while others fall foul of the dreaded biased referee…

Not only have the students written the stories, but they have also been involved in creating and marketing the finished product, which we hope you will enjoy reading as much as we enjoyed writing them.

I should like to thank Seth for being such a brilliant inaugural Author in Residence. He has been incredibly generous with his time, his contacts, and his enthusiasm, and the school is most definitely a richer place for it.

*Hattie Kimberley*
*Librarian*
*The Langley Academy*

# ALIEN ATTACK

*By Ryan and Rayan*

It's the final for a school named Wendagale High and their newest player, Rayne Wooney. He has weird, almost bruised green patches of skin and bright yellow eyes. He has abnormally big arms and legs - like they should be muscular, but they're not. No one at the school knew anything about him because he was quiet as a mouse and had no friends. He just kept himself to himself. Except when he was on the football pitch.

In a flash the match starts and the ball ends up next to Rayne Wooney's feet. Without thinking he runs off. He's already past all of his teammates, ignoring their shouts of "pass Rayne, PASS!" Rayne COULD pass. He COULD also cross the ball for a goal. But instead he decides to go for the risky option. He decides to go through all six defenders. One of them tries to barge him away but bounces straight off Rayne's abnormal arms. Kneeling in pain the defender calls out "AARGGGGH!!!". But Rayne ignores him. Rayne hits the ball through two of the other defenders' legs and breaks the ankles of the remaining three with his twisting and turning. He's face-to-face with the keeper! But will he score? Everyone is in a state of panic wondering how Rayne managed to do all that in two minutes, but that's not their biggest worry - the real one is how will he score? It's nearly impossible. The goal is too small. The keeper too big. Nearly impossible, just like his next shot…

◆ ◆ ◆

It was a normal day in Wendagale High when their football club was assigned a match against a rival football team in a month's time. Knowing how soon the match was, they started to practise straight away. It was going to be one of the hardest matches they'd have to play in their school's history. As they started to practise for the match they quickly realised that they were trash. If they didn't get any new players they'd lose by loads!

The next day the manager held tryouts to attract new people onto the team. Luckily, loads of students were willing to join. There was only one problem. They were all rubbish at football too! The school quickly lost all hope.
"Urgh man, we are never winning this!" exclaimed the manager.
"Don't lose hope, we can still do it," said one of the players. As the manager was about to give up, a mysterious boy walked in. He had brown skin and fluffy black hair, a red Liverpool kit on and blue football boots.
"Can I try out for the team?" he asked. "Trust, I'm great at football."
"OK, but you're the last one!"

They started observing his speed and they made him run across the pitch, and to everyone's disbelief he ran across it two times in under five seconds!
"OMG! WHAT JUST HAPPENED???" they all screamed.
"I don't even need to see anything else - that's a world record!" exclaimed the manager. "You're our new striker! What's your name anyway?"
"Beatrice Bangle", the new kid said.
"Well, Beatrice Bangle, you're our new main striker! We've got a match coming up, do you think you can help us?"
"Yeah, definitely bro."
"Great! Now we have a chance of winning. Get practising!"
"There's just one more thing," Beatrice said. Everyone stared at him. "There's someone else I know who can play football. He's called Rayne Wooney…"

Beatrice was so good that they trusted him and brought Rayne Wooney straight onto the team. Beatrice was up front and Rayne was in midfield. As the month went on, Rayne Wooney and Beatrice Bangle formed a firm friendship.  They got along really well and became best mates and were the best duo of teammates.

After a long month of practice it was the day of the match. Beatrice Bangle was just leaving home with his sports bag slung over his shoulder when he suddenly started to feel nervous. But then his manager rang him and said, "You're the best on the team. We all know you can do it so get here quick and don't let me down, champ!"

Beatrice got a rush of confidence as he neared the ground. Luckily it was a really sunny day and he had a huge bottle of water. Once he got to the match he saw the rival team - they were double his size but seemed way more stupid and unskilled; he knew he could do it.

They got in position and the match started… The other team, Rambooney FC, started with the ball and they passed it back to their midfielder who decided to boot it straight into Rayne Wooney's face. Rayne saw what was coming and dodged it quickly. His teammate Marandin controlled the ball with an amazing touch and passed it to Beatrice Bangle, now standing at left-wing, who started to dribble upfield towards the goal. It was all going well until he realised he had no one to pass to and the goalie was tall and muscular.
"How can I score this?" he questioned himself, but he had to try so using all his might he slammed it with as much accuracy and power as he could muster…and the goalie saved it.

BUT IT REBOUNDED!

It was his chance, but TOO SLOW! The opposing team took the ball and played it all the way back to their goal. Now he could see how he should play against this team. What was needed to score was TEAMWORK. If they stayed close together then whenever they got the chance they could pass it together and eventually shoot for the top corner furthest away from the huge goalie.

With the new tactic in mind, the team spread out across the pitch and started to pass to each other more often. Marandin had a bad touch but Rayne Wooney took control and passed to Beatrice Bangle, who back-heeled it quickly to Marandin, who passed in front of the goal for Rayne Wooney to head into the top corner, just slipping it through the goalie's hands…

GOAL!

The first of the match, and it gave them a big advantage. But as the game started over the other team ran like the wind to the other side of the pitch and chipped the ball over their own goalie and into the top corner, levelling the match at 1-1.

Everything started to go downhill for Wendegale High from then on. After that impeccable goal by the opposing team everyone lost hope and they were not playing at all well. Even Beatrice Bangle and Rayne Wooney were misplacing passes! The crowd had looks of disappointment all over their faces.

It was soon 2-1 to Rambooney FC and everyone assumed that they would win the match, but Rayne wasn't finished yet…They couldn't lose. He'd make sure they wouldn't lose, even if it cost him everything…

As the seconds ticked away Rayne decided to reveal his actual form and before the eyes of a disbelieving crowd he turned into an alien that could not be stopped. His skin became purple and scales grew from his back with cat eyes on top of them. The other team screamed, "Ref!! This ain't fair!"
"I've never heard a rule about no aliens on the pitch - play on!" the referee replied.
In his alien form, nobody could stop Rayne Wooney. He scored one goal, then two, then three, then four, then five, then six, until the score was 7-2 and Wendagale couldn't be beaten.

After the match was finished, Rayne Wooney, Beatrice Bangle and Marandin were voted the best on the pitch and got scouted for City and United where they would play with all the other top players. It didn't matter that Rayne was an alien. Nor that the other two were also aliens. There weren't any rules that said aliens couldn't play football. But despite the scouting they turned down the offers as they had learned all the secrets and skills of this planet's top sport. All this amazing fun had led the aliens to leave Earth alone and not destroy it as they had once planned. Instead they travelled back home to show all the other aliens the incredible new skills they had learned...

# THE LITTLE BOY FROM LAHORE

*By Saif*

With the whole world watching, millions of people with his name on their back, he steps up to take this free-kick. He shoots and...beep beep! The alarm wakes him up.

Let me tell you about Saiffey, a young academy player who is trying hard to make it pro. Today is the day, his last chance to make it for Spurs under 23s. Every moment of his life now fades into oblivion. This is the only day that matters. The only moment that matters. Making it would mean all the sacrifices were worthwhile, such as leaving his family behind in Pakistan to chase his dreams of being pro in England.

Saffiey heads towards the bathroom. To be a pro, you've got to look like a pro, dress like a pro, have the attitude of a pro. Dream big - and he did just that. Dreams about Lambos and Rolexes accompanied the passion of the footballer. *You've got to be loved. You've got to do whatever it takes.* This was his mantra.

Now it was time to kit up. With pride he slips the pristine white Spurs top over his freshly slicked hair. His spanking red, green and purple Nike boots were next and finally his comfy black gloves. He takes one last glance at the mirror before he leaves his house and flashes an arrogant smile. He slides into the fresh leather seat of his BMW and as quick as a flash he is there, leading the line, up front on his own.

In the 54$^{th}$ minute, Johnny the technically gifted midfielder plays a through ball into Saiffey, who delightfully chips the keeper and knee slides so powerfully that you could swear the world shook. After 90 minutes of intense, blood-curdling work, they win 1-0.

Saiffey exits the pitch with a smug grin across his face, which becomes even bigger when he's intercepted by the manager, Mr Nash.
"You did good out there kid, Spurs want you!" he exclaims. Saiffey accepts graciously but deep down he always knew he had it in the

bag.

Back in the changing room his teammates discuss the latest from Spurs. Apparently their star man Akram is out all season with a torn ACL. Saiffey knows what this could mean. When the time comes, he will be starting up front.

Before he knows it, it's gameday. Saiffey and Johnny begin to feel the nerves tumble in their stomachs and their hearts beat fast. They stare out with their mascots. Saiffey can hear the mumbling of the captain Chris telling him: "This is your chance make it count. And with that the whistle blows.

The Commentator bellows over radios and TVs around the world: *'Saiffey goes on a solo run and gets taken out for a pen! Johnny steps up and sticks it bottom left and they run off to celebrate. Johnny hits the corner flag, then the game continues. Half time occurs and the game starts off with Johnny picking up the ball and playing a through pass and Saiffey hitting it top corner.'*

The game finishes 2-0. Saiffey becomes an internet sensation overnight and instantly gets shot into the limelight. The next game is a semi-final against Preston North End. This is now or never for the boy from Lahore. As pressure in his young mind builds up the game begins. It's pretty close coming into the 87th minute - until the young and hungry Saiffey drives through the heart of the defence and calmly puts it through the keeper's legs. Spurs make it to the final!

The pressure. The pressure on young players nowadays is so much and for Saiffey, with all his arrogance, confidence and bravado, it is no different. He thinks back to Bukayo Saka, the young England star who missed a penalty and was relentlessly abused for it. What if the same thing happens to him? It's as if he can see into the future.

The final. 89 minutes in and cheers go around the ground. They have been awarded a penalty! With trepidation Saiffey approaches the penalty spot feeling the heat of a million eyes stabbing into his back. He is petrified. So much so that his heart thunders in his rib cage. Breathe. Just breathe. hear

The little boy from Lahore, with a million names on his back, takes the kick. And then ...

# THE BOY CALLED ISHAK GUIZEM: TRUST THE PROCESS

*By Amir, Hassan, Ishaq, Maksymillian and Adam*

"Come on, lads!" Ishak Guizem shouted. "Come on, get the ball from them."

"No," said Pratham.

"They are too tough for us!" the team said.

Every day at school lunch Ishak and his team called Langley Legends went to the school's astroturf to play a peaceful game of football. But every day the tough boys in the older year stole Ishak and their friends' ball and played roughly. All the tough boys were academy ballers and one even played for the Tottenham youth team. Those boys would kick the ball out of the fence sometimes. If Ishak or his friends tried to tell them off or complain then they would end up in hospital. That's because the academy ballers would beat them up after school, so no one dared to tell them off.

Every day at the astroturf, the same thing happened. So the Langley Legends decided not to go to the astroturf at lunch, but instead to come to school early and go to the MUGA, where they could play games of football until school started. Rather than getting bullied at lunch, the boys sneakily used that time to go to the school gym so they could work on their stamina and physical strength. Then, after school they would go to their local park and play football until sunset. After sunset, they would go to their local chicken shop and share three meals between all eleven of them due to the lack of money they had.

It was there that they decided they'd play against the academy ballers. And beat them.

Ishak knew they had to prove themselves before playing a match against the tough boys. So, they decided the top eight players between them must go to a 6v6 tournament at Slough Town FC. Ishak himself chose the team to play in the tournament. He chose Adam in goal, Tanveer in defence, Hassan in midfield, and himself and Amir up top. His substitutes were Aakarsh, a midfielder, and Amanveer, a defender.

It was tournament time. They made a strategy: win or lose they would play for fun. With that style of play the lads were so successful that they won a medal! Also, Adam, Hassan, Amir and of course Ishak were invited to play for Slough Town. Ishak and the other three who got the invitation decided to tell their school teammates, so they could ask them if they should join or not. Their school teammates encouraged them to join because then they would get even better and could one day match the academy ballers.

The four boys did just that. They didn't even know how they got picked for Slough's best team, but they knew that if they wanted to be a GOAT it was something they had to do.

"Come on, lads," Ishak shouted to Hassan, Amir, and Adam as they ran around in the yellow and blue of Slough. "Don't think those skinny boys are better than you." Slough had signed the boys on three-year deals, which meant they were 100 percent staying at the club until they got to the age of 16.

The boys started regularly for Slough, helping them to get promoted twice. Slough Town fans could not imagine these youngsters would have that much talent. They marvelled at their close control, their confidence, and of course their amazing skills!

When the boys' contract ended with Slough Town they got many transfer requests from clubs all over the world. There was so much choice! Agents scrambled over each other to offer them incredible deals. But the boys knew there was no point in joining a team where they would be benched the whole game. The boys also knew they had to separate themselves from each other and focus on their own game if they were going to improve even more.

So, the boys chose their teams:

Adam signed for Nice and decided to play for Poland.

Amir signed for Sevilla and decided to play for Germany.

Hassan signed for Feyenoord and decided to play for the Netherlands.

Ishak signed for Roma and decided to play for Algeria.

The boys had to say goodbye to each other as they were going separately to France, Spain, Italy and the Netherlands. This could be the last time they would see each other, but they knew one thing they had to fulfil on their bucket list: to play against the academy ballers. They knew that now it would be an easy win for them, but they had to trash them to make up for all that had happened in the past.

The academy ballers accepted the match gleefully. They didn't know about all the work the boys had been putting in.

The match started with the boys playing without any pressure. They knew it would be an easy win for them and all four scored lots of goals. The academy ballers got angrier and angrier. They tried to kick and foul the boys but they were too quick for them! All of those hours in the gym and training at Slough Town had made them untouchable. The highlight of the day was when Hassan played the ball to Ishak and he shot a bicycle kick right into the top corner!

The boys didn't even celebrate. It was now *too easy*.

After they trashed the academy ballers, Ishak said goodbye to his childhood friends and looked forward to joining Roma. Ishak flew to Italy to get his medical done. Strangely, José Mourinho came especially to pick Ishak up. José Mourinho told the world in his interview that he had seen many clips of Ishak playing for Slough

Town and that he thought he could make good chemistry with Paulo Dybala up front.

Before Ishak could debut for Roma, he got called up to international duty for Algeria at the World Cup qualifiers. In Algeria's group stage they had to top it to go to the World Cup. In their group they had Namibia, Kenya and Zimbabwe. With Ishak up front they beat Namibia and Kenya easily, and then they drew against Zimbabwe.

And so they made it to the World Cup qualifier group stage! In the World Cup qualifiers for the whole of Africa, Ishak was the top scorer, leaving behind the likes of Sadio Mane, Mo Salah, Riyadh Mahrez, Osmihen and many more African stars. And what did Ishak do? He shrugged it off like it was nothing. This is what training to beat the academy ballers had prepared him for.

When Ishak arrived in Italy his teammates treated him with huge respect. But Ishak knew he still had a lot to learn to be a GOAT like Pele, both Ronaldos, Messi, Maradona, and his personal favourite: Zinedine Zidane.

José Mourinho announced the team for Roma's first league match, against Gerona.

"I know you will be amazed I chose Ishak over Tammy Abraham," he said, "I chose him because I think Ishak has more stamina than Tammy. Tammy will still be playing every game, but mainly from the bench."

José Mourinho had faith in Ishak and it was time to impress him - even though Ishak knew it was hard for José Mourinho to be impressed. Ishak felt happy yet nervous at the same time. Still, he had to do it. To be the next Zidane.

The match started with Belotti curving the ball to Ishak, but Ishak overthought and overcomplicated his next touch. The ball ran out harmlessly for a goal-kick. After 20 minutes Paulo Dybala had a one-v-one with the goalkeeper, but he passed it to Ishak who had an open goal. It was wide open! All Ishak had to do was roll it in. But sadly, again, Ishak tried something special, and again, he failed. Mourinho rolled his eyes. The pattern continued all the way until the 70-minute mark when Gerona had a counterattack and scored. The Roma fans had lost patience with Ishak already!

They became so angry that they made a chant about Ishak saying 'get lost skinny boy'. This made José Mourinho even angrier with Ishak. He called over to Tammy Abraham and subbed him on for Ishak.

After the game, which Roma lost, Ishak sat alone on the bus to the hotel. Through the bus windows he could hear people swearing at him outside. None of his teammates spoke to him. José Mourinho wouldn't even look at him. Ishak thought that this was the end, already.

As soon as they got to the hotel, Ishak skulked off to bed. Before turning out the lights, he checked his phone. Bad idea! People were all over Instagram talking bad about him. On TikTok, they made bad edits of all his worst moments from the game. Ishak really now thought this was the end.

But out of the blue, just as Ishak was drifting off to sleep, a call came from Djamel Balmedia. Ishak answered it, stunned. Balmedia asked about what happened in the game, then told Ishak that it didn't matter as ups and downs happen. Balmedia also told Ishak to believe in himself and to keep working hard, because if he did then one day he would become a GOAT.

As expected, Ishak did not play in the next game or any other game for Roma for four years straight. He only played the warmup matches. He got paid less than his contract said he would and everything was going awfully for him. Even though he was still young, he felt so bad. Even worse than when the academy ballers bullied him. Like he was useless. Like he'd never be a proper footballer. And certainly not a GOAT.

Luckily, the World Cup was coming, and with no doubt he was in Algeria's team due to their wonderful coach who kept him motivated all the time, even when he thought it was the end. When Ishak played for Algeria he felt free. Not like at Roma, where he always felt nervous. And at Algeria, he played his best football. He was Algeria's star player, their top scorer and their captain. He knew this World Cup could be special for him.

The World Cup started with Algeria playing against Brazil. Brazil were massive favourites and, as expected, Algeria lost the match. They made it much closer than everyone thought, though. It was a hard match for both teams with Brazil eventually winning 2-1.

Guess who scored for Algeria? Of course, it was Ishak, with a banger of a free-kick.

The Algerians knew it wasn't the end as their neighbours Morocco once made the World Cup semi-finals. If they could do that, then maybe Algeria could do even better…

Maybe they could be the first African, Arabic and Muslim country to win the trophy…

With this mentality they came on the pitch for their next game against Mexico. This was also a tight game. It was 0-0, until right at the end of the game where Algeria charged forward in a counterattack. Ishak screamed for the ball, and when he received the pass he made no mistake. He scored to win Algeria the game!

This made them second in the group. They knew that they had to win against South Africa to go through. In the changing room before the game you'd think that they were nervous? But no. Ishak remembered Slough Town. He remembered the game against the academy ballers. He remembered how calm he felt. How he played without pressure. And so he did the same thing. Algeria won the game 5-0. Ishak scored three, Mahrez scored once and Benrahma scored a last minute penalty.

After the group stages finished, Ishak was the top scorer. That would show Mourinho! But Ishak told himself that there was no point in being happy now as he still had more games to go in the World Cup. The job wasn't done yet.

Because standing in the way was a familiar face. A very familiar face. Hassan, and his Netherlands team…

# FOUL PLAY

*By Sophie*

*1: Why Are You Following Me…*

Finally, the school day had ended. Everyone in year 7 and everyone in year 8 gathered on the football pitch. They were going to play against each other in a football match to work out which was the better year. For such an important match, they were going to need a brilliant referee. Alice put her name forward, but in the end everyone decided that Jack should be the referee. Alice stormed off in a sulk, not that anybody minded. They were all too focused on the game.

The game officially kicked off at 3 o'clock in the afternoon. Year 7 took the ball and started off with a great kick.

All of a sudden, Jack called a foul.

Everyone was wondering who had committed the foul, but they didn't have to look far. They all turned to look at Sophie.

"I only kicked him once!" she said.

All around her, people were startled. They looked around to see who Sophie had kicked.

Rayan lay on the floor. He was not even hurt but rolled around, pretending to be in agony. Sophie got put onto the side while another player went in as Rayan got up and continued. The match restarted and soon everyone was completely involved in the game. Well, almost everyone.

Sitting on the side, Sophie was getting more and more bored. Eventually, she became *so bored* that she decided to sneak away from the match.

Luckily nobody noticed.

Nobody apart from one person.

Rayan.

Rayan acted as if he was hurt and needed to leave the pitch. He lied. As soon as he was off the pitch he went and followed Sophie. By the time she'd reached the dark corridors of the school, Rayan caught up with her.

"What are you doing here?" he asked.

Sophie turned around slowly, not noticing her hands.

"Why are you following me?"

## 2: Bloody Hands

After Sophie had asked why Rayan had been following her she looked down and noticed through the darkness the blood on her hands.

"Ahhhhhh!" Sophie screamed. "How is there blood on my hands? I'm not bleeding!"

Rayan pointed behind her. And then they both screamed.

Luckily nobody heard because of the football match.

And nobody else knew about the murdered body on the floor...

## 3: Murder Mystery

"Who should we tell?" Sophie asked.

"No one," Rayan said.

"Why though?"

"Because if we tell anyone they will think that we did it."

"But who is it?"

"W-w-why don't you turn on the lights?"

Sophie reached nervously for the switch. Suddenly the room was flooded in light. The pair turned to look at who was there.

Jack.

The referee.

"Oh no!" shouted Rayan.

"What?" Sophie turned to look at him.

"That's Jack, the *best* referee," he said. "Why would anyone want to kill him?"

"Don't worry. We'll find out who did this."

## 4: Detectives Sophie and Rayan

"Look, he was hit with a sharp object in the stomach," Sophie said. "I guess it pays off taking criminology as an extracurricular club."

"So, it must have been a powerful strike. Let's look around to see if we can find any clues. We might even find the murder weapon!" Rayan responded. They started to look for clues. Sophie crouched down and looked under lockers while Rayan looked in the cubbies.

"Nothing so far", reported Rayan. They kept looking, and looking, and looking. Then Sophie spotted something!

"Hey, over here!" she called excitedly. "Look, a piece of paper."

"What does it say?"

Sophie unfolded the paper.

## I <u>See</u> You Found My Note.

## I'm <u>Watching</u> You.

*5: I'm Watching You*

As soon as Sophie read the note she looked straight up at Rayan.

"What do we do?"

"We could run," Rayan suggested.

"No, because if we run someone will see us and walk in here and then they'll see the dead body and think we did it!" As Sophie read over the note again, she noticed that the word <u>watching</u> was underlined along with the word <u>see</u>. "Hey, 'see' and 'watching' are underlined. What do you think that means?" she called.

"I don't know. How is he watching us?" Rayan called back. As soon as Rayan spoke, Sophie looked up and spotted the CCTV camera.

"Look! It might be on the CCTV – no one looks at those cameras anymore!"

"Yeah, it could be, but how can we access it? They normally lock the site manager's room."

Sophie thought again.

"Wait! **I** have a key! I completely forgot – I have my Daily Morning Messenger key. Let's go!"

## 6: The CCTV

Sophie and Rayan walked as silently as they could out of the back of the building.

"Let's hope no one goes in there!" Rayan said. As soon as they were clear, they started to run towards the CCTV room to check the cameras.

"Wait! Stop!" Sophie suddenly shouted, skidding to a halt. "The letter said the killer could SEE us. They're probably in the CCTV room watching us right now! It's a trap!"

"So let's catch him then," hissed Rayan.

"No, because he could double back us and say we killed Jack."

"OK, we won't get him, but let's look through the windows."

They crept up to the building and peered in through the windows…

They couldn't believe the sight that met their eyes!

The killer wasn't a 'him' at all. It was Alice, the female referee!

"So SHE's the killer," whispered Rayan. "She must have been jealous of Jack!" Quietly, they snapped a picture of Alice and then ran back to take one of Jack's body, before hot-footing it to the police station to show their evidence.

The police needed no more convincing. Blue sirens descended on the school. As soon as she heard them, Alice tried to run. But she wasn't quick enough. Alice was arrested and charged with the murder of Jack Kavinsky.

Sophie and Rayan got justice for Jack.

As they left to go back home, Sophie high-fived Rayan.

"Well done partner!" she said, "This could be the start of a brilliant detective duo…"

# THE PHANTOM FOOTBALLER

*By Ms Chanter*

"Amrit, Ellie, can you grab the footballs from the PE store cupboard?" requested Ms Greensmith with her shrill tone that pierced every student's eardrum. Eagerly, they skipped along towards the cupboard, down the old, white-painted brick Victorian corridor. Their footsteps echoing behind them. Fizzle fizzle shhm. The light flickered and suddenly went out.

"It's probably one of the boys," whispered Amrit.

Continuing with caution down the cold, lifeless corridor, the girls reached the PE cupboard door.

*Boing, boing boing.*

The unmistakable sound of a ball bouncing on polished school flooring, could be heard behind them. They froze suddenly, catching each other's eyes and slowly looked back.

Empty.

Returning to the task at hand, Amrit reached for the chilly silver handle of the PE cupboard door. Precariously, she stared into the darkness. The faint smell of must and sweat hit the back of her nose, choking her throat and making her feel uneasy. She fumbled around the inside wall for the switch. ON. But the light didn't turn on. She frantically began to switch the light, back and forth, on and off, to and fro but with no avail.

*Boing, boing boing.*

There it was again, this time closer than before.

*Boing, boing boing.*

"Jeez Amrit, hurry up. We need to get out of here," strained Ellie.

A clear look of panic was written all over her. Amrit didn't have a choice. She would have to go into the cupboard in the dark and find the balls. Hesitantly, she stepped inside, nearly slipping on a loose rounders bat. Feeling her way over sacks of cricket balls and stacks of hockey sticks, she reached the back shelf. Reaching up to the top of the unit, she pulled down the sack when simultaneously a ball fell out, hitting her, and the door to the cupboard slammed shut.

Amrit, grabbed the sack and tumbled towards the door.

"It's not funny, Ellie," Amrit bellowed.

Ellie instantly opened the door and protested it wasn't her. Amrit was about to argue, but her eyes were drawn to the figure behind Ellie, in an old school football kit, doing knee ups. The only thing was, she could see straight through him.

He stopped. He turned to look at the girls. Before they had the chance to run he…

# THE FATAL FOOTBALL

*By Rachel, Katrina, Maya and Lacey-Mae*

*1: Rachel Claw*

I was sitting in the changing room during half time with my team and suddenly I heard a BANG! It was so loud. I thought I couldn't possibly be the only one who heard it but I was wrong.

"Hey Maya did u hear that?" I asked.

"No, what are you talking about, are you OK?" replied Maya. I was confused. How could nobody have heard that sound! But I couldn't let that ruin our game.

"Yeah, I'm fine, don't worry," I sarcastically responded. Maya didn't notice.

"We can do this guys," Lacey said excitedly. "Let's smash the other teams. LET'S WIN THIS TOURNAMENT!"

*2: The Amazing Goalkeeper*

During half time me and the rest of my team were celebrating our latest goal when all of a sudden I felt a sharp pain shoot through my chest….Then it struck me: I'd been so caught up in the game that I was late in taking my medication! I looked through my bag and realised my pills weren't in there!

Confused and full of pain I desperately asked my teammates if they'd seen them. They said they had no idea where the pills were. Slowly, slowly I started feeling worse and my eyes blanked out, even as the sound of yelled concerns reached my ears.

In excruciating pain I finally woke. Long, ugly drips were connected to both of my arms. I didn't know whether to be happy or sad. I was alive. But I wasn't there with my team. I didn't even know if they had won or not! Nor did I know how I came to be here. The door opened and a nurse came in. She walked to my bed and injected something in my arm. What was it?! I was confused but I couldn't speak because the injection took effect. I was slowly fading away… it was dark and I couldn't see. Everything faded to black…What was happening? Why me?

Relief. I woke up again, sweating, feeling uncomfortable. I don't know what that injections did to me, nor HOW I ENDED UP HERE! The door opened again and it was my mum. I was so glad she was there.
"Oh, my darling, what happened!" said my mum, panicking.
"I don't know, I think I lost my pills. I'm so sorry."
"Aw no, it's fine, honey. As long as you're okay then that's fine," said mum with a slight smile.
"Thanks, mum. Love you. How was the game did we win?"
Mum looked at me with disappointment. I didn't know what she

was going to say…

## 3: Lacey Haze

I was super excited for the tournament. LET'S WIN THIS! I can't lie, I was a little nervous and I didn't think it would go to plan, but I hoped I was wrong.

SPOILER ALERT!
I was right…

As we were in the changing rooms our amazing goalkeeper, who was actually called Amazing Goalkeeper, suddenly keeled over. It looked like she was having a heart attack! She didn't know why and how it happened and neither did we?!

There was only one thing to do: we rushed her to the hospital and gave her over to the medical staff.

We haven't seen her since…We heard that she woke up but then something else happened. Complications, or something…I was scared. It looked like someone had done whatever they'd done on purpose. It could have been any one of us (except me, OBVS). I felt as if something else bad was going to happen.
"I hope she's OK," said Rachel.
"We basically lost the tournament because of that," said Maya.
"No, they should redo the tournament," I said Maya. I always made the most sense out of my friends.
"No, they won't," she replied.

We were in the waiting room at the hospital when suddenly the TV screen flashed up with BREAKING NEWS. The cameras rushed to a reporter who was at the pitch we'd just played our tournament on!

*"Around 1 at a football tournament a goalkeeper called Amazing Goalkeeper was found to be poisoned by taking the wrong pills. We are soon to investigate the situation. There remains controversy as some people didn't think it was a big deal and that they should still continue the tournament. However, it was one of Amazing Goalkeeper's teammates who pushed to find the culprit. This has been John speaking."*

Three weeks later further news came. Amazing Goalkeeper didn't make it. Someone had switched her pills on purpose. This wasn't a mere medical emergency. It was murder! the tournament was postponed until further notice. The police had to investigate EVERYWHERE. But they couldn't find anything. Weeks later, the investigation was closed with no answers.

It didn't sit right with us. Something had to be done.

## 4: Katrina

I couldn't believe they ended the investigation! They should have continued it. Maya nodded her head when I told her. IKR she said, it's so totally unfair. Still, I'm the goalkeeper now and I can be just as amazing as Amazing Goalkeeper. Maybe even better. But there was something about the way she said the first part. Like, her eyes flitted from side to side. She was so totally not convincing. So I stared at her, super hard. And I could see she grew smaller the harder I stared.

Then her face went pale.
And her mouth opened wide.
Her goalkeeper-gloved hands shot up to her mouth.
And she turned to run.
"I agree," a voice said from behind us. "It's not right. Because we've just found out the culprit. It was you..."

# THE GREATEST GAME

*By Raheem and Kalimullah*

And so the time is nigh. Mbappe. Messi. Immortality awaits one, and only one. Lionel Messi stares up at his final peak. Kylian Mbappe prowls in the foothills of greatness. From the Andes to the Alps, from the river plane to the banks of the ocean, the whole world wants to know the answer that one single question. Who is the GOAT?

From playing barefoot in the streets of Argentina to the world's greatest stage, this World Cup final is the most important match of Lionel Messi's life - of anyone's life. But in his way stands Kylian Mbappe, the French wonderkid. With pace to burn and the ability to devastate the most difficult of defences.

*Peep!*

The whistle sounds and the game begins. First touch to Messi. He controls the ball and delivers an outstanding pass to Angel di Maria, who shoots a mighty shot but alas! It collides with the crossbar and bounces high into the night sky. But wait! Messi swarms toward the ball, reacting quicker than anyone else. He leaps and the ball leaps with him into the net. A goal! Argentina are winning 1-0.

Led by Mbappe, France find their feet in the game. The tension grows. If the score remains, Messi will undoubtedly be the GOAT. In every break in play, you can feel the laser vision of Mbappe locked onto Messi. He does not want to allow this. For in just a few years, he plans to have won it all. To be even greater than Messi. To be even greater than Cristiano Ronaldo. He's already given Messi enough of a headstart. Mbappe won't allow Messi to win anything else.

This is the greatest show on Earth.

For Messi, it feels as if his life is flashing before his eyes. These moments are more impactful than death itself. From the corner of the Argentine magician's eye, a tear flows. He sees the ball again and chases it, his heart racing. He chases it again and again, chasing life itself. Chasing greatness.

# TAKING IT TO TIKTOK

*By Brooke, Jessica and Leah*

*Meet the characters...*

**Rosie**: *loves pasta. She's tall and exceedingly popular. Loves reading books, and films so many TikToks. Oh, she's also kind of famous...*
**Brooke**: *hates art but loves drama. Caring but a little bit weird.*

*Leah*: kind and welcoming. Likes football and hanging out with friends. Loves funfairs.
*Jessica*: kind, caring and very welcoming. Loves fairs, football and watching movies.
*Maddison*: kind and caring. Loves parks, probably because she's a football addict.
*Winnie*: she's crazy but caring, and loves hanging out with her friends (and playing football).
*Summer*: loves winter. She cares about her friends, to whom she's known as the most crazy one.
*Lilly*: dog fan and footballer. An addict who cares.

## 1: Football Girls

Rosie woke up from her bed and as she did every day, decided to check her TikTok to see what the latest trends were. When she got on the app all she saw was football, football, football (she hates football). But then she had an idea...

Her idea was to stop her friends from liking football so when they all hang out, they would not leave her out (and would stop posting about it on TikTok).

Just then her phone buzzed and she got a message saying 'hey want to come to the park and hang out?'. Since she was quite bored anyways, she decided to go to the park. When she got there the girls were playing football, just like usual.

Rosie said, "guys why are you playing football, weren't we supposed to hang out?"

"We're still hanging out, we're just playing football because we love football," replied Leah.

"Oh ok, but you know I hate football right!"

"We didn't think you were actually going to come but we can hang out in 10 minutes."

## 2: The Mess

10 minutes later and they were still playing football.
"Guys, it's been 10 minutes, why are you still playing football? We were supposed to be hanging out."
"Well, we're still playing because it's a tie, 2-2. Just give us another 10 minutes, I'm sure we will be done by then!" said Maddison.
"Oh, ok I'll come back in 10 minutes to see if you're done," said Rosie.
But ten minutes later they were still playing...
"Guys, it's been 10 minutes! Have you finished yet? I'm just going to go home if you're not going to hang out," said Rosie.
"Go home, we don't care. We're playing our second match if you couldn't tell!" Leah said angrily.
"FINE. I'll just go home now. You obviously don't care about my feelings, do you!" Rosie said with tears running down her cheeks.

## 3: The Fallout

When Rosie got home, she was still crying. She felt like all her 'friends' were users. She went on Tik Tok so that she could make new friends who didn't abandon her for football. After a bit of scrolling, some girls reached out to her. They liked football but promised to always include Rosie.Their message said: 'hey I've seen you at the park and your friends seem fake, do you wanna hang out with us?'

Rosie was really happy, but she'd never seen the girls before. Still, she replied saying 'yeah I would love to!'

Rosie met them and they were really nice. Her old friends were also there and they were still playing football! One of the girls Rosie had just met shouted at them saying "oi you lot! Why are you leaving your best friend out? You always play football and that is so rude because you are basically picking a sport over your best friend, wow. You never deserved her if you treated her that way." Maddison was so furious about what the girl said...

## 4: The Footballer Arrives in Town

Rosie and her new friends left the park, but little did Rosie know that one of the girls contacted a worldwide footballer (wow, that sounds like a dream). And even better, the footballer replied!

Later that day, the girl asked Rosie if she wanted to come to Hyde Park. She had a surprise for her.
'I love surprises,' Rosie replied. 'Of course!'
Once they reached Hyde Park Rosie was confused. "What's the surprise and where is it?" she asked, but one of the other girl said, "he's coming, just give him a minute."
One minute passed.
And then another.
And then he arrived!
"OMG I CAN'T BELIEVE YOU'RE HERE IN HYDE PARK, OMGG" Rosie screeched. It was Phil Foden! He introduced himself to Rosie and Rosie introduced herself to Phil. Phil then asked: "Do you like playing football by any chance?"
What could she say? Rosie felt upset. She couldn't escape this stupid sport!
"I don't really like football, but I play it and ever since today my friends basically picked a sport over their own friend, and I was so shocked that I collapsed into tears," she told him. "My new friends felt so bad for me. They tried to make me happy by telling me that those other girls don't deserve such a nice and pretty friend who

they probably used for fame. They said that if I tell the world about those 'friends' then they would learn their lessons."

Phil felt bad for Rosie straight away. Of course he'd seen her TikToks before and knew who she was. So he asked: "do you all want to play a match with me? I know you don't like football but we can make it fun." That sounded OK to Rosie, and her new friends all accepted.

Rosie couldn't believe it! They all had a wonderful time with each other. Hours went past so quickly that before she knew it the sun had set and it was 8pm. They all said their goodbyes then and went home - kind of. They all went to the same home for a sleepover at Rosie's home. Rosie was so excited because she finally didn't feel all alone, and had some devoted friends.

Once they got to Rosie's house, Rosie said "should I make a TikTok about all the girls that were very rude to me then tag them and say they should learn a lesson. But then I guess I don't wanna be rude." The girls said yes do it! It wouldn't be rude because they deserved it.
"Like I can't even believe what they did, like, I wouldn't do that," said one of her new friends. "Football always ruins best friend relationships."

## 5: The Sleepover

Rosie then proceeded to make the TikTok about them to tell everyone how fake her old friends were and how to avoid fake friends. Once they finished editing the video they uploaded it but since it was very late they all decided to go to sleep. Little did they know that when they uploaded the TikTok Phil Foden commented on it straight away. Then so did other footballers. And more celebrities. Their TikTok was blowing up overnight.

When the morning came they had their breakfast and Rosie

decided to check her phone like normal.
"OMG YOU WILL NOT BELIEVE," she screamed.
"Rosie, what happened? Tell us!" replied Jessica.
"You know the TikTok we made?"
"Yeah, what about it?"
"Well, look at this…"

# THE BIASED REFEREE

*By Riley, Jayden and John*

Some referees are good. Some referees are bad. And some referees are biased.

This referee was really, really biased. Only, he thought he was really good.

Riley, Jayden and John didn't think he was really good. That's because they were playing in the match that he was refereeing. They were all playing for Langley, and the referee was being biased against them.

It was making them furious.

The referee had already given five red cards and seven yellow cards to Langley, and it was still the first half. He'd even booked John for *sneezing*.

"Get up the pitch," shouted Langley's manager to his defence.

*Peep!*

The referee blew his whistle and ran over to the manager. He reached into his pocket and showed the manager a red card too!

The crowd had seen enough. At half time they left the stadium. All 200,000 of them!

Langley were losing 1-0. If they were unable to win, it would be devastating for them.

In the dressing room, Langley's players were throwing their bottles and bags everywhere. They were furious at what was happening! They were also worried, because they were losing and didn't think they'd be able to win with such a biased referee. They'd have to send the referee off! It was their only chance.

Well, not their only chance.

Langley had a new student who looked a bit older than everyone else. He had come from Argentina on foreign exchange, and it turned out he was pretty good at football. He was called Lionel Messi.

When they subbed Messi on, everything changed. It was so hard for the other team, Ditton Park, to get the ball off him. They started to two-foot him. A crazy player came out of nowhere and picked up Messi and chucked him over.

"Aren't you going to give a foul?" shouted John at the referee. The referee just gave John a dirty look and waved play on. Anger exploded in John. He punched the referee so hard that it knocked him out. The referee had to be taken from the pitch on a stretcher!

But there was no replacement referee.

The game had to restart. Jayden got control of the ball and began to get tekkie, using the inside and outside of his right foot to work his way toward the goal. Then he spotted Langley's Portuguese star, Cristiano Ronaldo, and laid it off to him. Ronaldo only had to guide it into the net. 1-1!

With five players sent off, and Lionel Messi still hurt, Langley were actually drawing! But time was running out.

There were just two minutes left when Riley picked up the ball on the right wing. He played it across to Jayden, who found John. John dribbled past the last defender and all of a sudden was one-on-one with the goalkeeper. He swerved to the right and the goalkeeper leapt at him. John screamed as he felt the contact. The goalkeeper had been nowhere near the ball! It had to be a penalty. The Langley players all turned to the referee to scream for a penalty.

But there was no referee there...

# GOING BIG IN BRAZIL

*By Billy, Jaiden and Liam*

Let us tell you about our team. We're bad. Really bad. But you'll never guess what?
We've got a chance to play in a tournament.
In Brazil!
And even better, the winners get £100,000.
That should be able to buy our team loads more equipment!

The tournament starts and even though we're bad, something crazy happens. We all click. We get through our first round, then the next round, and before we know it we're in the final against Ronaldo Junior's team!

Ronaldo Junior shouldn't have to cheat, right? Wrong! Ronaldo Junior and the rest of his team are the biggest cheats going. We try our best and early on Jaiden scores. We all go crazy with our celebration! But then Ronaldo Junior does a great BIG dive and wins a free-kick. Even though it's 45 yards out, we build a wall. But when the free-kick comes it's so good that it goes straight over that wall and straight into our net. Ronaldo Junior is good at cheating. Turns out he's *really* good at free-kicks.

It feels like the referee is allowing them to cheat. They make a really dirty challenge in the area, so dirty that Kalokoh has to go off injured. The referee waves play on. There isn't even a yellow card!

The other team are all so fast. They get to the ball so quickly. It's really hard to keep up with them. As our team gets more tired, they seem to stay the same. If anything, they even get quicker!

It's tough work to chase Ronaldo Junior. But then something unexpected happens. Billy gets fouled in their penalty area. And then something even more unexpected happens. The referee gives a penalty!

There are 95 minutes on the clock. This could be the final kick of the game.

Jaiden steps up. He takes a deep breath as he tries to shut out the crowd and their boos.

The whistle blows.
He steps forward…
And misses!
But wait…
There's a VAR check.
They think the goalkeeper must have been off his line. Liam is sure he was! And yes, the VAR confirms it.
So Jaiden steps up again.
He shoots…
And this time it goes into the top corner!

Ronaldo Junior only has time to take the kick-off. The final whistle blows and suddenly the rain pours down.

Then something strange happens.

One by one, the other team's boots start sparking and smoking. We look closer and realise they've all got electric boots. No wonder they were so quick!

Now the crowd have realised too and they're booing them, but then they're cheering us. Then booing them.

The other team realise they're rumbled. But remember, they're cheaters. So what do cheaters do? Well, they either cheat. Or they get aggressive.

Ronaldo Junior is the first one to throw a punch. His teammates all pile in and a massive fight breaks out. Billy, Jaiden and Liam throw punches wherever they can. Even fans are on the pitch fighting! Billy karate kicks someone and it turns out to be their goalkeeper! But before he can do anything else, he sees that Liam is getting beaten up. Him and Jaiden run to Liam, then kick the person off him. Someone has the referee in a headlock!

"We need to stop fighting, guys!" Kalokoh roars from the sidelines. He's still on the stretcher after getting fouled. "We need to think of the money. £100,000 is a lot."
But nobody hears him. They're all too busy…

# THE LIBRARIAN'S REVENGE

*By Seth Burkett*

"Erm, what are you doing?"

The boy looked up, startled.

"This is my library and I will not tolerate messing about," the librarian said, her voice thick with authority. A hush descended on the room. All around, school pupils' eyes were trained on the exchange between the librarian and the boy.

"Nothing," he replied.

"It's not nothing," the librarian retorted. "You're pushing your friend, you're eating and I can also see a phone. This is a library, a quiet place for reading or playing games. You have no book, and you have no games."

The boy's cheeks flushed. He didn't like being told off, yet nor did he like being embarrassed in front of his friends. As far as he could see, he had two options: apologise, or fight back.

"It's a free world," he replied, quietly at first, but then with the increasing confidence that comes from being surrounded by mates. He pushed back his chair and got to his feet, rising to his full height of six feet. If he was going to fight back, he was going to do so by impressing his classmates. "And I'm going to stay here. You can take your books and stick them -"

Before he knew what was happening, the librarian stormed over. The boy may have towered over her, but that proved no problem for the librarian. In one swift movement she lifted him by the collar with more force than anybody watching thought possible. The boy's mouth was still open, quivering as if he were a fish fresh out of water, gulping for air. His black Air Max trainers dangled helplessly six inches above the floor. He tried to finish his sentence, but no matter how hard he tried the words just wouldn't come out.

"Out!" the librarian commanded, pushing him toward the exit. "And don't think about coming back. You're banned!"

◆ ◆ ◆

"I've got a problem with those boys," the librarian said to her assistant. She clasped a mug of milky tea tightly in her hands. Breaktime was over and the pupils were all back in their classes. For now, it was a chance for the librarian to relax.
"Everyone here does," the assistant replied, reaching for one of the biscuits on the table in front of them. "They need to be taught a lesson. Someone should put them in their place."
"Yes," the librarian replied absent-mindedly. Her gaze was fixed in the distance. It was as if you could see the cogs whirring in her brain. The assistant shrugged her shoulders and reached for another biscuit. She'd learned that when the librarian became lost in her thoughts, it was best to leave her to her own devices. She'd come back into the room eventually.

"What do those boys like doing?" the librarian eventually asked.
"Same as most people in this school: football on the astro."
"Do they go out there a lot?"
"Every lunch. I think most of them want to become professionals in the future."
"Yes...yes I'm sure they do,' the librarian replied, sitting back in her chair. She took a sip from her mug.
"You used to play football didn't you?"
"A little."
"A little! Didn't you play for the national team?"
"I dabbled,' the librarian replied. 'I don't like to tell many people."

"So none of those boys will know?"
"I presume not."
The pair locked eyes with each other. The same idea had come to them at exactly the same moment. It was brilliant! Genius!

◆ ◆ ◆

By lunchtime, the librarian and her assistant had hatched their plan. They'd recruit the best unknown footballers around the school, then challenge the troublesome group of boys to a match on the astro. The librarian would play in goal: the position where she'd won all 34 of her national team caps. The assistant would play in midfield, because she liked running up and down the pitch so she could help the defenders and the attackers. That meant there were still three places to fill: one defender, one midfielder and one striker.

"Do we still have budget to get an author to do some workshops?" the assistant asked.
"Why do you ask?"
"Well, we always get authors in for World Book Day. It hasn't been World Book Day yet so I presume we still have some money knocking about. Why don't we use that money to get a footballer in to the school instead? We can tell the pupils they're an author. They won't be able to tell the difference."
"Perfect. There are loads of authors out there anyway. We can just *say* they've written books about football."

The librarian spent the next hour contacting professional football clubs. She devised an email explaining the situation and adding in that it'd look excellent for the football club's community engagement profile. Although the footballer would have to pretend they were actually an author and had never kicked a ball before. They couldn't be too well-known, either. As long as they were professional, ideally in the lower leagues, and wouldn't be recognised. Meanwhile, her assistant gathered all of the library helpers in a huddle and asked if any could play football. It turned out that many could, and several even played for football teams outside of school. She selected two: a year 7 called Ivy and a year 8 called Alex. They all agreed that the four of them would make a great team. None of the troublesome boys, all in year 9, would expect them to be any good. How wrong they'd be! All they needed was a star: a fifth player.

◆ ◆ ◆

The librarian sighed. Another email. Another rejection. Sure, they could still find a fifth player from elsewhere, but the librarian didn't just want to win. She wanted to win by so much that the boys would never mess about in her library ever again.

◆ ◆ ◆

The librarian took a deep breath in and a big breath out. The group of boys stood before her, laughing and joking in the maths corridor. None had seen her yet. In her mind she ran through what she was going to say. It had all made so much sense before, but now the whole plan seemed…a little far-fetched? Had she let herself get carried away in the moment? No, it was silly. It was -
"What are you looking at?" The boy scrunched his eyebrows at the librarian, daring her to say something back. His mates instantly assembled behind him, backing him up. They may have been in year 9, but the librarian noticed how they were all so big. Already, some had facial hair. To her eyes, they seemed to be teenagers trapped in the bodies of men. She took another breath, composed herself, and then spoke.
"You all like football, don't you?"

◆ ◆ ◆

The boys all laughed incredulously when they heard the librarian's offer. Of course they'd take on the librarian and her team on the astro. Why not make a whole event of it? Invite the whole school. The more people who'd see the better. They were certain they'd win.

Their attitude made the librarian even more determined.

And when she got back to her desk, that determination skyrocketed. A response! From a footballer. And even better, a footballer who played football in a different country. Yes, of course, they'd pretend to be an author. How hard could it be? They'd read a book once.

The librarian smiled. Everything was coming together perfectly.

◆ ◆ ◆

Steph Blake didn't look like an author. She looked like a footballer. Her body was all muscle and no fat. She moved with an air of confidence that comes from sending crowds wild every weekend. But at least she hadn't worn her club kit to the school.

With the librarian's coaching (and PowerPoint slides), Steph managed to give two workshops on writing. Whenever she became lost for words, the librarian made sure to mouth what Steph should cover next.
"That was mint," Steph said after the second workshop. She was beaming. "I've learned all sorts today. I'm going to go home and read, maybe even become an author. It doesn't seem too hard."
"Yes, yes, yes. Books are great,' the librarian replied 'But about this match…"

◆ ◆ ◆

The astro: where legends are made and reputations destroyed. Where top bins are struck, Brexit tackles fly in and five-star skills come from those in scuffed Kickers and Hush Puppies. Whatever you do, keep your legs shut. A nutmeg is worse than a goal. Today, it felt as if the entire school had descended on the hallowed turf. As the librarian looked around the crowd, she even spotted faces from the primary school across the road. There were teachers, catering staff, pupils, parents. Everyone who was anyone was out there, all waiting for the latest legend to be created. The next soul to be taken.

"Is it because they think I'm an author?" Steph whispered.
"Partly," the librarian replied. "But mainly because they're all excited for the game. Remember what I said. Play as if this is a normal game. Whatever happens, we cannot lose."
At the other end, the group of troublesome boys were far less serious. As the librarian, her assistant, Ivy, Alex and Steph

huddled together, the boys booted balls into the air and high-fived the crowd. In their heads, they'd already won.

The boys started the game by knocking the ball back from kick-off. Before their midfielder could even take a touch, the 'author' was on them. With one extended right leg, Steph stole the ball and played it wide to the assistant, who whipped a cross in to Alex. Too long!
"Cor, that author can really play football," said someone on the sideline.
"Lucky she can play football," someone else replied. "Because earlier she told me that she didn't know what a noun was."

The first goal soon came for the librarian's team. Once again Steph won the ball in midfield, but this time she decided to dribble instead of pass. She dribbled past one player, then a second, then a third. Before she knew it she was one-on-one with the keeper. She made no mistake, chipping the ball into the net.

"Can you believe they're losing against the librarian and an author!" the crowd laughed. The boys hadn't banked on such a result. Losing hadn't seemed a possibility. With renewed energy, they pushed and pushed. Brexit tackles began to fly in, some as high as their opponents' waists. As time went by, they became more and more aggressive. On multiple occasions the referee had to stop the game to flash yellow cards in their direction. Half time came and went. Still, the librarian's team held on to their 1-0 lead. Steph continued to win the ball and pass it forward. Alex continued to be a nuisance upfront. The assistant continued to support the attack and defence. Ivy kept her shape. And the librarian leapt and dived and caught and punched. Nothing was going to beat her.

Nothing until her assistant lost possession in midfield. The boys' team counter-attached quickly. Ivy was hopelessly outnumbered. Steph was trapped upfield, Alex nowhere to be seen. Ivy positioned herself left, then right, then as the ball was played she charged and leapt through the air. Too late. The ball had gone, but the boy was still there. The two bodies tumbled onto the astroturf, crashing through the crumbs of black rubber.

Penalty!

They could have no complaints. It was a stonewall penalty. Blatant. The librarian accepted her fate. The boy picked up the ball, pushing away his teammates, and placed it on the spot. The crowd, previously raucous, were now silent. All attention was on this moment. There was hardly going to be any time to restart the game. The lunch bell was about to sound.

This was it.

The librarian tapped her right post, tapped her left post, and then placed both hands on the crossbar. She puffed out her chest, then spread her arms to make herself appear as big as possible, and the goal as small as possible. She thought back to all those moments the boy had messed about, made her life hell.

The boy smirked. This was a chance for him to get his own back on the librarian. He'd hated being told off. Hated being removed from the library. It was his school. He could go where he pleased. Do what he wanted. He took four gigantic steps back, then two smaller ones to the left, and waited for the whistle.

He stared at the librarian. She stared back. Both determined.

They were surrounded by silence. The crowd watched on, hypnotised by what was playing out in front of them. And then the whistle blew, and the boy charged forward. He wound his right foot back, then struck the ball with as much power as he could possibly muster. The librarian dived in the direction of the ball, stretching her fingers to their very limits.

She'd show the boy. She'd never been more sure of herself.

# FIGHTING FIRE WITH FIRE

*By Chloe, Lois, Sienna and Zara*

One hot, sunny afternoon, Chloe, Zara, Lois and Sienna were playing football. Before they knew it, Zara and Sienna had got into a fight! It all started when Sienna kicked the ball into Zara's face and Zara got mad.

"Sorry!" Sienna said, but Zara didn't accept the apology. So Sienna tried again: "Look, I'm sorry. It was all an accident."

"No! I do not care. It was on purpose, I know it was." Zara rolled her eyes. Chloe and Lois came to see what was happening. They were shocked to see that the pair of them were arguing.

"Guys, what's going on?" Lois asked.

"Yeah, why are you guys having a fight? Like, it's just a game, chill," Chloe said in a scared way because she didn't know what Zara was going to do next.

"I said sorry and she won't forgive me. I honestly don't know why she's acting like this?" Sienna said.

"I don't care! She started it by kicking the ball in my face, it was on purpose!"

"Guys, stop. I'm going to the shop, does anyone want anything?" Chloe said in a way to change the conversation and stop them fighting.

"I'm coming, Chloe, I really don't wanna be here anymore with these two fighting," Lois said.

They waited for Zara and Sienna, but neither said a word. They just stared at each other angrily. So Chloe and Lois shrugged their shoulders and went.

"Listen, I don't want to argue with you anymore, OK?" Sienna said. "I really like being ur mate so let's stop."

"No, I'm sick of you, it hurt." Zara pointed at her face, which already had a big bruise from where the ball had hit it. "It's bad you know, you're so annoying."

"Look, I can't do this anymore. You keep shouting and blaming me. OK, I'm done." A crazy look came over Sienna's face. She drew her fist back…

"Wait, what-" Zara began to shake with fear.

"Sorry, Zara…"

Sienna threw her fist forward and connected with the other side of Zara's face. In her shock, Zara crashed to the ground as Sienna ran away.

"Guys, the shop was rubbish-" Chloe and Lois froze as they saw what was happening. Their jaws dropped.

Lois was the first to react.

"ARRRRRGGGGGGHHHHHHHHH!" she screamed and ran away.

Chloe did the opposite. She rushed toward Zara.

"OMG, Zara? ZAR?!" Chloe cried. She rang the ambulance and told them all that had happened. She searched desperately for Sienna but couldn't see her anywhere.

*NEE NAW NEW NAW*

The ambulance screeched into view and a paramedic rushed out.

"What happened here?" they demanded.

"Our friend has been attacked!" Chloe cried.

"OK, we will check the CCTV for a full -"

"SIENNA!" cried Chloe. "She killed Zara!"

## THE NEXT DAY

Chloe, Lois and Sienna all met up the next day.

"Hey girls," Chloe said brightly.

"Hi," said Lois.

Sienna didn't speak.

"Sienna, is all OK?" Lois asked.

"Yeah, you're too quiet to be you, everything good?" Chloe asked.

"Yeah, all OK," Sienna said, though she looked sadder than usual.

They ordered coffee and cake.

They had a chat.

And then they told Sienna they knew what she'd done.

"What?" Sienna said, dumbstruck.

"We know you killed Zara, own it." Sienna's face flushed red. She breathed lots of quick, tiny breaths. There were tears in the corners of her eyes.

"You know, I did kill her but-" she burst out, then quickly covered her mouth, as if she hadn't meant to say anything. "Don't tell ANYONE! Get it? Shush!" Sienna said. Her eyes were daggers.

"OK, but first," Lois pulled her first back and smashed it into Chloe's temple.

"OMG, Lois! You shouldn't have done that!"

"You did? So why can't I?" Lois had a crazed look in her eye.

"I HAD A REASON, OK!" Sienna yelled.

"Whatever. Now we are a team you have to get over it. I joined the force of death. Now let's get out of here before we get caught."

## 5 YEARS LATER

"Who were Zara and Chloe again?" Lois said, joking around…

# THE BALL APOCALYPSE

*By Salahuddin*

In the distant future, aliens with supernatural football abilities bring havoc to the football community as they destroy the soccer players we love.

Messi loses the World Cup after failing to score past the devious hands of the alien goalkeeper.

Salah and all of Liverpool's players are zapped of their popularity.

Ronaldo, the best of all time in my opinion, has been…actually, he doesn't really change, except he cries even more after Portugal are left with an even heavier defeat when they face Morocco.

As you can see, all is not well…

*…Until a time machine is developed in a scientific laboratory. The aliens, knowing the danger of such a device, attack the laboratory but cannot find the machine. Instead, the machine is left to rot, waiting for Earth's saviour.*

◆ ◆ ◆

"Get down, we could be abducted by aliens!" Mum giggled, expecting me to laugh along. I didn't.

"Mum, that's not funny!"

Hello, my name is Zack. You may be wondering why have we come from a distant future to a somewhat normal setting. Well, it is because this is my story of how I saved the world from aliens, so let me carry on.

"Well, I sure hope that secondary school is funny," Mum said. I had just started high school, middle school, secondary school, whatever you want to call it. Hardly anyone from my old school came to my crummy new school, Greenwood High. My whole family had gone to Greenwood High - even my great, great grandparents - I wouldn't be surprised if our family owned the school.

"Thank you for the support," I said sarcastically as I went out of the front door and into a new world, my world: the teenage world. I strapped myself to my bike and hurriedly pedalled. The chain whirred round, faster and faster, until I bumped into a crashpad of a guy. BOOM! The force threw me off the bike, which flew to the side of the road. I sprang up, dazed, then saw the guy's clothes. He was going to the same school as me.

"Hi, my name is Jone," he said.

"Hi, my name is Zack." I felt nerves building up in me.

"Do you wanna walk with me?" he said with a gentle tone. "We need to be careful with all these aliens about."

"Yeah, I don't mind." I clambered back onto my bike and Jone ran behind me as we hurried toward school. But when we got to the front gate we found it closed. That was odd. Jone looked confused. We turned and walked to the other entrance, past the dumpyard. The back entrance was through a crooked fence with a hole in it.

"Argh!" Jone pulled his foot up to his hand. He'd stubbed it against a large rock.

"I'll get rid of that," I said, trying to help. I picked it up and threw it over the wall into the dumpyard.

And then it happened.

There was an enormous explosion and the fencing around the dumpyard all fell, leaving just one object. A cupboard, just big enough to fit a human body in, with a clock on the front…

# THE SWITCH

*By Marcel, Osamagbee and Yousef*

## 1

Our story takes place in a small town in Philadelphia. The buzzer sounds…

It's 72-69 to Ohio State University. One minute left on the clock. And OSU with the ball. Their player sets himself, takes a shot…and misses. Jass, the tall, confident captain of Philadelphia State University, catches the rebound and takes possession.

He dribbles the ball down the court, dodging left and right through defenders. Just before the three-point line, he pulls up, takes aim, and shoots.

The crowd goes silent.

The ball swishes through the net.

And then everyone goes crazy.

The crowd chants "MVP! MVP!"

Until a player from OSU passes the ball down the court. The

receiver goes for a layup, from nowhere. In the knick of time, Philadelphia's Maleek appears and steals the ball! But he isn't done there. He passes the ball to El-Taka. El-Taka lobs the ball to Iqbaldinhio. Iqbaldinhio shows off his fast skills, dribbling past everyone in sight. He alley-oops the ball to Osa in the air, as Osa palms the ball and dunks it.

The crowd chants, "OSA, OSA, OSA!!!"

But again, OSU come back. They score, tying the game at 74-74. The clock ticks down. These are the moments when legends are made.

30 seconds left.

The ball gets thrown to Jass, bringing the crowd to their feet. You can see how eager Jass is to impress, to make this game-winning shot. He charges toward the basket.

"Dunk!" comes a cry from the bench.

He follows their instruction. Just one metre from the basket, he crouches down and then floats up toward the rim. He reaches toward the hoop.

Suddenly, he feels a striking pain in his rib.

An opponent has launched himself into Jass's chest, sending him flying towards the ground. As Jass hits the floor his vision becomes blurry. Screams from all around pierce his eardrums. Through the panic, he sees his coach running toward him. But then everything fades to black.

## 2

The wind blows against Jass's skin. Slowly, his eyes begin to open.

The sun shines down into his eyes. From somewhere, he can hear a faint whistle sound.

El-Taka stands above Jass. He's wearing a different kit from before as he stretches his hand towards Jass. Jass notices his vest is now a t-shirt. His basketball socks now knee-length socks. And are they shinpads?
"Get up, the game isn't over!"
Jass reaches out and takes El-Taka's hand. Once on his feet, he looks around.

Wait, what?

His eyes flash as he realises that this is not the basketball court. No, for starters there is grass, not wood. There are goals, not hoops. It's not a basketball court. It's a football pitch.
"Where are we?" Jass asks. "W-Why are we playing football?"
"Ha, funny one ‚Jass." El-Taka laughs before running off. Jass feels nothing but confusion, Again, he looks around the bright green, grassy field. In the corner, a scoreboard flashes.

*OSU 2-1 PSU*

*FINAL*

"This is the season finals!" Jass announces to himself. There's shock written all over his face. He checks the scoreboard again. There are 30 minutes left of the match.
What will Jass do...

3

As Jass brings himself to a run, his teammates stare at him in awe.

Jass shouts for a pass and a spark of hope is lit in their eyes! They pass, and then Jass passes. Even in the haze of this situation, Jass can see that his team is playing with confidence.

The ball flies forward once more. Jass jumps and wins a header. Suddenly, El-Taka is through on goal. He makes no mistake. 3-1!
When the final whistle blows, the crowd go wild. They celebrate and take the trophy.
"Another one for the trophy cabinet!" roars El-Taka.
"Hey, let's party!" shouts the PSU football coach - a man Jass has never seen before.

◆ ◆ ◆

Later that night, Jass finds himself outside the manager's house in a smart outfit. El-Taka is ahead of him, already talking excitedly about the night ahead. As they go through the door, they're met by waiters, all holding drinks. Jass gladly accepts, but as he sips the drink his head begins to feel heavy. His vision blurs. Suddenly, he collapses. El-Taka runs toward him, but before he arrives everything has faded to black once again.

## 4

Jass's eyes slowly open. Beams of sunlight shine down through the windows. Until a dark figure steps into his vision, covering the sun. Jass squints. It's his coach. Not the football coach. His old coach from basketball. The coach's muffled shouting slowly clears up as Jass comes more to his senses.
"JASS, JASS!" The coach is shaking him. "GET YOUR HEAD IN THE GAME!"

Jass rubs his eyes and realises he's back in the basketball match. Confused, Jass steadily gets to his feet and looks around.

"What happened?" Jass asks.

"You alright, can you play on?" the referee asks, ignoring his question.
"I'm good," Jass quietly peeps. That's good enough for the referee.

The game carries on.

It feels to Jass like an eternity since he last played basketball. Maleek shouts his name and Jass looks up to see the ball flying towards him. He instinctively kicks the ball.

PEEP!

The whistle is blown. Foul! His teammates stare at him, confused at what just happened.

Jass hangs his head. It still feels as if he's on the football pitch.

He apologises to his teammates and vows to use his hands. Until the ball flies in his direction and he sticks his foot out once more.
And again.
And again.

Jass shakes his head and curses himself but it's too late. His team have already lost the match. He's cost them the game.

## 5

The team disappear to their homes, disappointed after the loss. Jass takes a taxi back and when he arrives he collapses on his bed. He's still so frustrated at what happened in the basketball match, and so confused at what happened with his blackouts. He tosses and turns and eventually sleep comes.

At around 7 in the morning Jass wakes up to a loud bang.

The wind feels cold, the sun burns through the curtain and lights up his eyes. He has a horrible headache banging against the inside of his skull. Groggily, Jass gets up and opens his closet to get out his clothes for the day. He feels a strange tension while opening the closet door. And once the door is open he sees why. Lying on his folded up clothes is a massive golden trophy. Jass reaches out and lifts it closer. There's text on the base.

*PSU, winners of the university finals*

"So all of this was real?" Jass asks, rubbing his eyes once more…

# THE DYLAN CASE

*By Alex*

T hump. Thump.
He stood on the cold, plasticky grass, drenched in sweat and rain.
87th minute.
1-1.

He watched, inside the safety of his box, the ball sailing to Maaka, to Sharma. From foot to foot, edging closer and closer. Past the defenders, from the corner post, shot straight into the box.

A jump.
A goal.
A cheer.

He failed. Turning to the referee, he shot a questioning look - whether it was valid or not. The referee shook his head.

1-2.

It was all over.

They had come all this way, only for him to mess it up, to lose them the trophy. Collapsing to his knees, he looked up, towards the skies, as if asking whatever God there was a singular question: Why?

## *Three hours later*

He woke up on a cold stone floor, wet with his tears. Looking up, he expected to see his door, the comforting mahogany of his room. But he didn't. He saw a metal door. He went to stand up, but couldn't. Metal shackles dug into his ankles. Panic spread across his body. Suddenly, the door creaked open and a hooded figure looked down at him. They turned around, muttering: "He's awake."

"Good," the voice within the darkness responded.

## Four days later

*DYLAN MOORE - Owls' goalkeeper MISSING!*

The detective slammed his head into the table. Russel Branco, a detective for the Langley police department, had been assigned to the Moore case. He'd discovered that Moore was forcefully taken from his home, with no resistance, probably drugged. The trail ended there - Russel had spent two nights attempting to find any form of evidence, anything that would lead him somewhere. He just needed *something*.

What he *really* needed was the forensics department, and he had spent the last three hours arguing with his superiors as to why this case was so important, and why he 'should waste' the forensic teams' time on 'just another high-profile kidnapping'. Now he looked up, fingers ready to sling another aggressive email back at his boss.

## Two hours later

He stood inside a fancy house, sweating from the heated wooden flooring. He never thought Dylan made this much money. Where did he get it all from? He shook his head - that was irrelevant.

He waited outside a fancy mahogany door, carefully standing in between the scuff marks on the floor. The crinkle of plastic faintly sounded from within. He had succeeded. The forensics team was inside Dylan's room, analysing the room for any traces of anyone. Anything.

Slam.

The door shot open, and the forensics team came running out, carrying all their most expensive equipment.

"BOMB!" one screamed, charging head first through the open door. The team leader carried on running, but then slammed into the front door - it was locked! Russel stood there, stunned. The heated floor would ignite and set the entire building ablaze. They had to get out - NOW.

Russel looked around frantically. Was this where they died? Their final resting place? Would they be blown to smithereens in a fiery grave, their bodies unrecognisable?

No, Russel could not let that happen.

Thud, thud, thud. He ran across to the room with the bomb. Grabbing the largest object in the room - a small safe to store evidence in - he ran out, downstairs, back to the front room. Holding it in both hands, the rounded corners of the metal box digging into each palm, he slammed it into the lock of the front door.

And again.

And again.

Nothing happened.

Spinning around, he glanced at the kitchen. No. But wait - he recalled the floor plan of this building, the same one he'd spent nights analysing. Yes, now he remembered the tool cupboard near the front door. Sprinting into the hallway, he looked around, throwing doors open in desperation, his heartbeat rising with every step.

Until at one of those doors his eyes lit up. He saw what he thought was salvation.

A whole chainsaw.

He grabbed the end of it, wondering why a goalkeeper of a mildly famous football team had a tool cupboard, let alone a chainsaw in it. The forensic team winced and cheered in equal measure as they watched Russel rev up the chainsaw and begin sawing the deadbolt out. With a resounding thunk, the deadbolt fell onto the pavement outside. Russel kicked open the door, crying out as it flung into the wall. Without pausing, he sprinted out, running towards the police cars outside screaming "BOMB!".

Russel and the forensics team stopped outside as the gates flung wide open. Once safe, they panted for breath outside the building, preparing for the explosion that would ignite all the evidence.

"Are you sure it was a real bomb?" Russel asked the forensics' lead. "Absolutely, it was even ti-"
BOOM.
An ear-deafening explosion echoed out with a blinding lick of flames consuming the entirety of the house, ruining all the evidence that could help lead them to Moore. They collapsed onto their knees, feeling the heat of the flames hitting them at full force. All of the leads were gone, all they had left was the players to interview.

So that's what Russel did.

But first, he had to endure screaming. A whole lot of it.

"HOW STUPID ARE YOU?" the plump man in front of him screamed. It was his boss, a man who loved nothing more than putting his underlings in their place. "YOU IDIOT. YOU LED THE FORENSICS TEAM INTO A TRAP AND WASTED THEIR TIME ALONG WITH MOST OF THEIR EQUIPMENT. THAT EQUIPMENT WAS WORTH MILLIONS OF POUNDS!"
"But I didn't know there was a bo-"
"LOOK AT MY FACE."
Russel was already looking at his face.
"DO I LOOK LIKE I GIVE A DAMN?"
Russel shook his head.
"That's what I thought," his boss muttered, walking off.

◆ ◆ ◆

Russel pulled the chair out from under the metallic table shining in the glare of a harsh, ancient tube light. A man sat there, wrists shackled to the solid aluminium table that was bolted into the floor. Beads of sweat dripped down his forehead, diamonds of fear edging their way down. His hands, despite being tied down by cold, gunmetal steel, shivered and shook with dread. His name was Adam Perez, and he played right forward for the same team as Dylan.

"I- I want a l-lawyer," Adam groaned.
Russel leaned back.
"Mate, I'd much rather you didn't. I doubt you're guilty, so it won't hurt to just talk."
"O- ok."
"So. What... er... happened?"
"O-on the d-day it happened, I-I was at home, w-with my girlfriend watching a m-movie."

Russel made a mental note to interview his girlfriend.
"So, you had no idea about the disappearance?"
"N-none."
"Hmph. OK."

Russel unlocked Adam's wrists with a key.
"Go away."
Adam bumped into the table while standing up, and walked out of the room as quickly as he could.

Russel sighed. It was going to be a long day.

◆ ◆ ◆

Click. The metal door swung open. A hooded figure walked in, sliding a bowl of… something with a wooden spoon shoved inside. The door shut, and the hooded man - or woman, he didn't know - unlocked the shackles on Dylan. A gruff voice, hoarse yet *familiar* sounded, telling him to eat.
Dylan laughed.
"Of course. Of course it's you," Dylan muttered.
The hooded figure's blue eyes shone as the sun echoed through a crack in the ceiling.
"Why?" Dylan asked.
The hooded silhouette said nothing. Dylan sighed, picked up the slop from his bowl, and began to eat.

◆ ◆ ◆

Russel was tired. His eyes flitted over to the clock in the corner of his screen – 4:32am.
He had been awake all night, searching through the archives, yellow books, police documents, even those creepy stalker fan forums that had somehow worked out the address of every single player on Dylan's team. Convenient, he thought, albeit illegal and

unconventional.

He had narrowed it down to two suspects.

There was Bryn Nielsen. As the team's striker, he had the highest chance of being the kidnapper.

Then, there was Trystan Jacobs. He was the captain of the team and could also have been the kidnapper.

He would search them tomorrow.

Russel walked around the damp, dark basement, slight drops of water occasionally dripping down from the ceiling – or was it the floor – above. He was unnerved but reassured by the weight and feel of the cold gun holstered in his back pocket. The torch in his hand flitted around as Russel tried to find anything incriminating in Trystan's house.

And then, in the corner of the basement, there it was.

A form of storage – somewhere to keep his… furniture? There was broken and abandoned furniture strewn across the left corner of the room. Russel walked towards it, examining each piece. There it was. Scuff marks on the floor, next to the strangely intact cupboard. Russel pushed it aside, and saw a gap in the wall, a hole, with stairs going down. Russel walked in.

Dylan was hungry. The hooded figure hadn't returned to give him his slop again. Along with that, he couldn't feel his arms. He was angry and confused. How could this happen? He didn't know how long he had been there for. Was he going insane? He didn't know. He closed his eyes. A blinding light shot itself through his eyelids, forcing them open. He rubbed them, to see a torch pointed straight at him from outside the cell.

"Don't worry. I'll get you out of here," the person with the torch said.

They lifted a radio out from somewhere and called for help unlocking the cell, and then in arresting Trystan. The person put it back, and started kicking at the door. Dylan smiled. He was safe.

Russel walked upstairs, moving towards Trystan calmly.

"You're under arrest for the kidnapping of Dylan Moore," Russel said.

An expression of shock appeared on Trystan's face. He seemed speechless. He never thought this would happen, and yet it had.

"It was perfect... How? How did you find it?" Trystan asked.

"You didn't wipe off the scuff marks on the floor. It was pretty easy, honestly," Russel replied, cuffing him.

"I'm not a very good kidnapper, am I?" Trystan responded.

"Or maybe I'm just a great detective…"

# ACKNOWLEDGEMENT

**I first visited The Langley Academy in 2022. It was a fantastic experience. As an author, I travel the country to give talks and workshops in schools, universities and businesses. It's no exaggeration to say that Langley was one of my favourite visits - and not just because of the great school dinners.**

Hattie Kimberley made me feel welcome immediately. With a neverending supply of biscuits and an insistence on washing up my mug between hot drinks, time spent in the library was a pleasure. Following introductions and refreshments, it was time to meet the pupils. I found them to be warm, engaging, and full of insightful questions. I only had an hour with each year group, but could have spent so much longer. Still, the highlight was to come: lunch on the astro. After showing a few skills, it was time to test myself in the energetic - and highly competitive - games that took place between tens of pupils and one ball. Credit goes to all of them that they held off doing their 'Brexit tackles' on me.

I left the school with a big smile on my face - which doesn't always happen!

So when Hattie got back in touch to ask if I'd consider becoming Langley's first Author in Residence, I jumped at the chance.

Meeting with Hattie and Katie Chanter, I quickly became excited by their idea of engaging pupils through football and writing.

Working with years 7, 8 and 9, we'd develop their creative writing skills, give them insight into the book process, and then get them to have a go themselves.

As you can see from the stories in this book, they embraced the challenge.

It's been wonderful to see their thoughts come to life. They've been full of energy throughout the process, often animated when talking about ideas close to their heart. We've played football matches with unique scenarios, brainstormed crazy ideas, and eaten plenty of biscuits thanks to Hattie.

Throughout the process, Hattie and Katie have been incredible. They've put in so much effort, always staying positive - even when half the room gets distracted by word games on the iPads, other pupils walking past, or those singing a TikTok song about a grey tracksuit...

Despite those tiny issues, the pupils have been a pleasure to work with. They're special, with some incredible talents in a diverse range of areas. Some have great potential with their writing. Others come up with ideas seamlessly. The way that they've worked together to achieve this book should be applauded.

I hope it won't be the last time that they put pen to paper.
I hope that this is only the beginning for them.
But most of all, I hope that they can be proud of what they've achieved.
They certainly should be.

*Seth Burkett*
*Author in Residence*
*The Langley Academy*

# MORE INFORMATION

**Learn more about The Langley Academy:**
https://www.langleyacademy.org/

**Discover Seth Burkett's other work:**
https://sethburkett.com/

Printed in Great Britain
by Amazon